BIANCA GUSENBAUER-HOPPE

TASTE & COOK
— WITH BIANCA IS(S)T —
IN VIENNA

"ISST" means BIANCA EATS and "IST" means BIANCA EXISTS
– so it's a German play on words!

Contents

Sides

Veggies & Meat

The essentials on sweet Austrian dishes

The Austrian sweet tooth

Traditional Christmas bakery

10 FACTS ABOUT *Vienna*

1 *1.9 million people* live here, spread over 23 districts.
Vienna's old city center is a WORLD HERITAGE SITE.

2 Districts are called by their NAME & NUMBER and follow an easy circular and radial system.

3 *Viennese cuisine* is a real brand. It is said to be the only cuisine in the world to be named after a city.

> SERVUS!
> = HELLO

4 In Vienna, people speak *German with a local accent.*
It's the second biggest city in the German-speaking world, after Berlin.

5 Vienna is known for its HIGH QUALITY OF LIVING.
In 2019, the Mercer Study voted Vienna the world's *most livable city* for the tenth year in a row, while in 2018 the British magazine "The Economist" ranked it number one for the very first time.

6

Austrians are proud of their COFFEE HOUSE CULTURE, which is also registered as an intangible World Cultural Heritage by UNESCO. Take the time to enjoy a leisurely coffee, lunch or dinner.

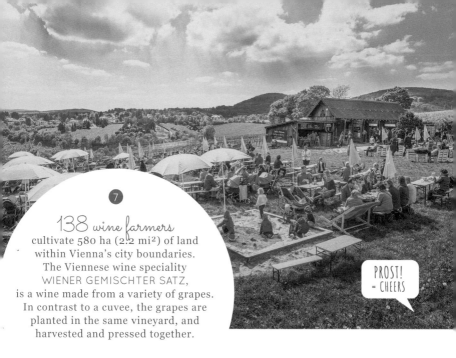

138 wine farmers cultivate 580 ha (2.2 mi²) of land within Vienna's city boundaries. The Viennese wine speciality WIENER GEMISCHTER SATZ, is a wine made from a variety of grapes. In contrast to a cuvee, the grapes are planted in the same vineyard, and harvested and pressed together.

PROST!
= CHEERS

The wine taverns serve their own wine and are called *"Heurigen"* and serve hot and cold food with regional wine.
The best tram lines for reaching the Viennese wine areas are:
#D NUSSDORF – Mayer am Pfarrplatz, Schübel-Auer, Kierlinger
#38 GRINZING – Müllers Heuriger and organic tavern Obermann
#31 STAMMERSDORF – organic taverns Wieninger and Christ

⑧ *Austrians love dancing!* Over 450 BALLS are held every year in Vienna. Most of these events usually take place in the first quarter of the year, between New Year's Eve and Mardi Gras. During that time, you'll see people wearing ball gowns and tuxedos in the streets, grabbing a late-night sausage snack after a night of dancing in imperial palaces.

⑨ *The Sacher Cake* is a chocolate cake that became famous world-wide. Visitors often line up in front of Hotel Sacher in the city center, where it was invented – SEE PAGE 62 >> , but it can also be enjoyed in every other coffee house.

⑩ The city's *sausage stands* – mostly small sidewalk kiosks – not only sell hot dogs but also wieners, Käsekrainer (cheese kransky) and fried sausage, and a whole range of culinary surprises. These are complemented by an impressive variety of beverages, from local soft drinks to specialty beers.

7 MARKETS IN VIENNA
you shouldn't miss on a Saturday morning!

Vienna is rich in markets and locals enjoy shopping. Particularly on Saturdays, it's become very popular to spend time there – to shop, chat and eat. Discover the richness and diversity of the Viennese markets!

It's best to GET UP EARLY, because some of the markets close around lunchtime on Saturday. DURING THE WEEK markets are usually open until 6 p.m., restaurants even longer.

Also, CHECK OUT THE TRAM LINES that connect the markets to other places of interest.

KUTSCHKERMARKT – a local high-end market!
This beautiful market offers an interesting variety of local and international goods. Enjoy a platter of cheese and a glass of wine in the middle of the market.

🚇 U6 Währingerstrasse or AKH

BRUNNENMARKT – gentrification at its best!
This lengthy market is a combination of bazaar and, on Saturdays, a farmers' market with local producers and growers. Enjoy the mixed atmosphere and lunch at RESTAURANT WETTER, which has large windows looking onto the market.

🚇 U6 Josefstädter Strasse

HANNOVERMARKT – a vibrant, authentic market!
This is an international market and even most Viennese have never visited it. Here you'll find authentic international food that caters to Viennese migrants and locals alike.

🚇 U6 Jägerstrasse, U4 Friedensbrücke

FREYUNG – organic market
This lovely little market on historic ground is only open from Friday to Saturday. Spare some time for a glass of wine accompanied by an excellent cheese or ham platter.

🚇 U2 Schottentor, U3 Herrengasse

GET UP EARLY & HUNGRY!

MEIDLINGER MARKT – *local and hip!*

This small market is the rising star and caters to Viennese from beyond the local district. Enjoy cheese, great bread, cake, lunch or dinner in one of the restaurants.

Ⓤ U6 Niederhofstrasse or U4 Meidlinger Hauptstrasse

ROCHUSMARKT – *small, but busy!*

Enjoy a coffee outside and check out the local seasonal produce, ranging from cheese to fruits.

Ⓤ U3 Rochusmarkt

KARMELITERMARKT – *slow food market!*

This market is famous for the special foods offered by regional producers. Enjoy the vibrant atmosphere on Saturdays only!

Ⓤ U2 Taborstrasse

Food sightseeing BY TRAM

Public transport in Vienna is fantastic!

Jump on a tram, relax, observe the locals and stop at one of my favorite spots. The colloquial name we use for our trams is "BIM", because of the ringing sound the tram makes when using the horn.

In order to get a LARGER PICTURE and a BETTER UNDERSTANDING of Vienna, you should definitely ride around the city on a tram. **Don't be afraid of getting lost** – it's super-easy to go back and forth by tram.

BEFORE YOU START YOUR RIDE, make sure that you first buy your ticket at an underground station because they're not sold on every tram or bus.

A SINGLE TICKET can be used for 60 minutes (as a one-way, not a return ticket) on all forms of transport, no matter how often you change from one form of transport to another within that hour. But you can also buy a ticket for a longer period - 24, 48 OR 72 HOURS - or DAY CARDS, depending on your plans, for unlimited use on all forms of transport.

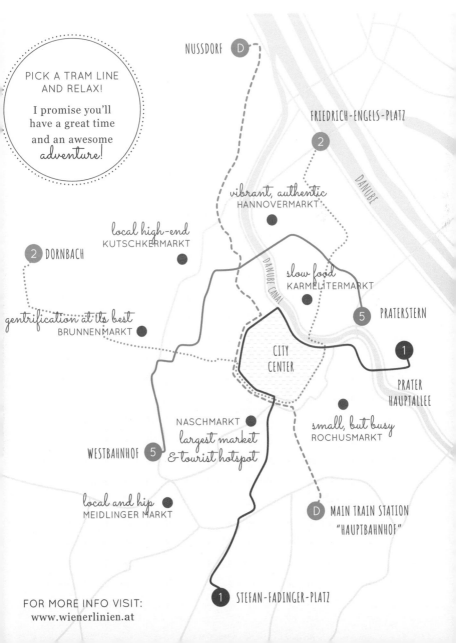

OVERVIEW OF TRAM RIDES & markets

PICK A TRAM LINE AND RELAX!

I promise you'll have a great time and an awesome adventure!

NUSSDORF D

FRIEDRICH-ENGELS-PLATZ

2

DANUBE

vibrant, authentic
HANNOVERMARKT

local high-end
KUTSCHKERMARKT

2 DORNBACH

DANUBE CANAL

slow food
KARMELITERMARKT

5 PRATERSTERN

gentrification at its best
BRUNNENMARKT

CITY CENTER

1

PRATER HAUPTALLEE

NASCHMARKT
largest market
& tourist hotspot

small, but busy
ROCHUSMARKT

WESTBAHNHOF 5

local and hip
MEIDLINGER MARKT

D MAIN TRAIN STATION
"HAUPTBAHNHOF"

1 STEFAN-FADINGER-PLATZ

FOR MORE INFO VISIT:
www.wienerlinien.at

1. HEURIGER SCHÜBEL-AUER
A winery that serves food and drinks either in the garden under the chestnut trees or in the quaint, old-fashioned restaurant.

2. NUSSDORF – Set off on a hike of discovery from this lovely little neighborhood.

3. PLACHUTTA NUSSDORF
Famous for its prime boiled beef, the restaurant Plachutta has a branch here too.

4. MAYER AM PFARRPLATZ – A short walk up the hill brings you to this famous and beautiful wine tavern.

5. KARL-MARX-HOF – Nothing to eat, but impressive to see. It's the most famous and largest social housing complex in Vienna.

6. WEINKELLEREI SCHLUMBERGER
This traditional Viennese sparkling wine producer offers tours of the cellar.

7. THE SIGN – The most creative cocktail bar in Vienna. Crazily good mixtures for later in the evening.

8. MAST WINEBISTRO – A must-stop for lovers of wine and food. A group of young guys is doing a great job providing an entertaining evening full of enjoyment.

9. GASTHAUS WICKERL
Another good option for traditional food.

10. SERVITENVIERTEL (SERVITENGASSE)
Don't miss this charming little area of tiny shops and restaurants. I even got my wedding ring there.

D — FROM *urban treats* TO THE SCENIC *wine district* OF VIENNA

On this *scenic tram ride*, enjoy a mixture of historical sites and traditional restaurants, finishing up in the picturesque wine-growing area of Nussdorf, where you can taste fresh wine and go on a rewarding walk up the hill.

11. REBHUHN – A beautiful traditional restaurant and a real institution in the neighborhood. It's received an award for the best Wiener Schnitzel.

12. RESTAURANT HANSEN – Downstairs in the old stock exchange building – a wonderland of flowers and food.

13. RESTAURANT GIORGINA
A hidden gem which you should try for lunch or dinner during the week.

14. ORGANIC MARKET FREYUNG >> PAGE 6

15. HOFBURG – The former principal imperial palace of the Habsburg dynasty is a must-see on your trip.

16. CAFÉ PALMENHAUS – A romantic restaurant and coffee house in the gardens of the Hofburg (15)

17. GMOAKELLER – A good traditional restaurant which also caters to guests from the nearby concert hall in the evenings.

TRAM RIDE
without a stop
40 minutes

18. RESTAURANT GRACE
A young team will surprise you with seasonal dishes.

19. CAFÉ GOLDEGG – A hidden treasure of Viennese coffee house culture. Just around the corner from Belvedere.

20. BELVEDERE – Is not only a magnificent Baroque palace but also houses one of Austria´s most valuable art collections, including Gustav Klimt's "The Kiss". In winter, you'll enjoy the quaint, colorful Christmas Market.

1 ENJOY amusement WITH LOCALS IN THE PRATER AND A GREAT beer garden

On this fantastic tram ride you'll find an *interesting mix* of traditional stops and urban treats. You'll enjoy relaxing hours in the huge natural park of the Prater, pass beautiful, hidden-away residential areas, enjoy the urban atmosphere, visit the old city center and finish up in the urban 4th district.

1. PRATER – Nowadays, the old imperial hunting ground is a great natural area for sports and fun in the amusement park or restaurants.

2. KOLARIK´S LUFTBURG – A unique spot in Vienna where you can enjoy organic traditional food and beer in a large beer garden or in the newly renovated restaurant. They're famous for their grilled knuckle of pork – a delicacy which should always be shared!

Interested in architecture?
3. The HUNDERTWASSER MUSEUM is on the way and well worth a stop.

4. WARENHANDLUNG – Just a short walk from the tram stop is this small shop run by two young ladies, where you can enjoy coffee and sample hand-crafted Austrian food.

5. RADETZKYPLATZ – A nice "round corner" with several good restaurants and bars, depending on what you're looking for. GARAGE serves excellent cold beer with fusion tapas. GASTHAUS WILD sticks to traditional food and CAFÉ MENTA serves Arabic-inspired food.

6. STRANDBAR HERRMANN – Was the first riverside bar in town and is still very popular during warm days.

7. Go down the stairs – in summer, both banks of the DANUBE CANAL are occupied by pop-up restaurants and bars.

8. O BOUFÉS – A great place for all lovers of natural wines to reserve a table. Enjoy fusion Greek-Austrian cuisine served family-style.

9. CAFÉ DIGLAS – Has two branches and is the best place to enjoy sweet Austrian dishes in a homely style.

10. UNGER UND KLEIN – A well-established, cozy wine bar, focusing also on Austrian wine. Stop by here – and enjoy cold cuts, relaxing hours and a tasty wine selection.

11. RESTAURANT HANSEN – Downstairs in the old stock exchange building– a wonderland of flowers and food.

12. RESTAURANT GIORGINA – SEE TRAM D >>

13. HOFBURG – SEE TRAM D >>

14. ORGANIC MARKET FREYUNG >> PAGE 6

15. CAFÉ ANZENGRUBER – A real institution among creative and normal people who enjoy this simple, old-fashioned, relaxed atmosphere.

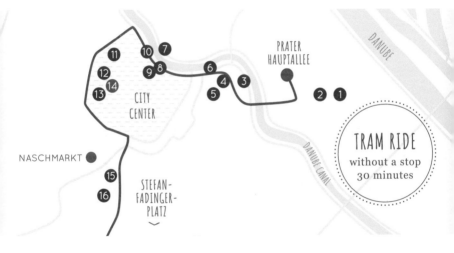

15. BABETTE'S – BOOKS FOR COOKS
A great place to shop for cookbooks and organic spices.

15. SZIGETTI SEKTCOMPTOIR – Enjoy choosing your glass of Austrian sparkling wine in this small bar. You can bring your own food from the nearby NASCHMARKT, which is the largest open-air market in town.

15. VOLLPENSION – A unique place in Vienna where retired people bake cakes and serve drinks in this always busy, shabby-chic café.

16. GASTHAUS UBL – A beautiful traditional restaurant where you can spend the whole evening.

2 DISCOVER *vibrant markets*, THE OUTSKIRTS OF VIENNA, & GLORY IN THE *night life*

Basically, you'll get *everything* on this tram ride!
You can go on a hike in the Vienna Woods, enjoy the Danube or take a swim in an old-fashioned open-air public swimming pool. On the way, you'll pass two lively markets and several excellent restaurants and local favorites.

1. AUTOMAT WELT – A refurbished old restaurant with a wonderful bar, loved by locals for its excellent selection of drinks, great food and relaxed atmosphere.

2. MONTE OFELIO – We just love this cozy place, which is owned by Sicilian brothers. Well worth a visit!

>> Walk to the Augarten from here. SEE TRAM 5 >>

3. KARMELITERMARKT– The area around this market is very hip, and several restaurants on and around the market are well worth a stop. >> PAGE 7

4. VEGANISTA IV – Ready for some dairy-free ice cream?
A great address for ice-cream lovers.

5. MOTTO AM FLUSS
Urban and hip. Enjoy sunset, breakfast or dinner on board a ship.

6. HUTH GASTWIRTSCHAFT – Excellent traditional food in the city center.

7. LE BAR – Ready for some sparkling? Enjoy a glass of champagne or a great cocktail accompanied by bar food in this small bar of Hotel Sans Souci.

8. TÜR 7 – You have to ring the bell to get into this speakeasy, which serves excellent cocktails.

9. FROMME HELENE – A local favorite for traditional cuisine and much-frequented by the guests of the nearby theater.

10. CAFÉ FLORIANIHOF – A wonderful quiet spot for a coffee break or a glass of wine.

11. PIARISTENPLATZ – A very picturesque square with a summer garden belong to the neighboring restaurants, including fantastic pizza.

12. CONCERTS ALONG THE U6 – If you're interested in young night life with live music, walk along the U6 line from old run-down CHELSEA to the B72.

13. BRUNNENMARKT AND YPPENPLATZ – Especially on Saturdays, you can enjoy a great mixture of Arabic and local hip culture here. >> PAGE 6

13. WETTER – This is my favorite market restaurant, serving excellent modern Italian food.

13. STAUD – Is a well-established local brand of Viennese jams and pickles. It has its shop at Yppenplatz.

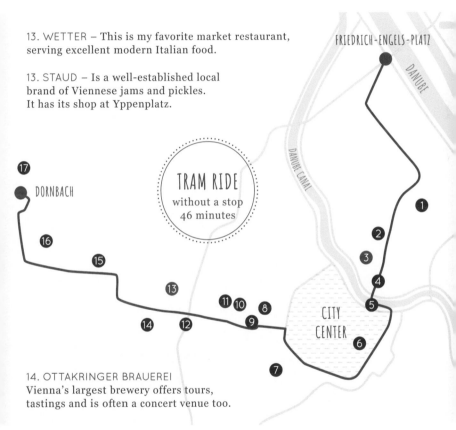

TRAM RIDE
without a stop
46 minutes

FRIEDRICH-ENGELS-PLATZ

DANUBE

DANUBE CANAL

DORNBACH

CITY CENTER

14. OTTAKRINGER BRAUEREI
Vienna's largest brewery offers tours, tastings and is often a concert venue too.

15. GELBMANNS GASTSTUBE – Go local with traditional Austrian food.

16. KONGRESSBAD
Wonderful old-fashioned open-air public swimming pool.

17. VIENNA WOODS – Discover the outskirts on easy hikes and catch glimpses of Vienna through the trees.

12. GASTWIRTSCHAFT SCHILLING – A really wonderful traditional restaurant which serves local food for locals. Good option for a schnitzel experience.

13. SCHREINER'S ESSEN UND WOHNEN
This hidden gem in a busy street is only open from Tuesday to Friday.

TRAM RIDE
without a stop
33 minutes

DANUBE

DANUBE CANAL

PRATERSTERN

CITY CENTER

WESTBAHNHOF

SEE ALSO TRAM 1
FOR RECOMMENDATIONS
IN THE PRATER

5 THIS *tram ride* WILL SHOW YOU JUST HOW *diverse* VIENNA IS!

You'll *enjoy relaxing* in the extensive grounds of the Prater, local markets, fine-dining restaurants and the wonderful Augarten park, which locals regard as a green extension to their homes. Experience sunset in the Augarten, taste excellent craft beer, the best pastries in Vienna or a vegan lunch.

1. SUPERSENSE – The analog answer for digital natives. This wonderful spot is well worth a visit. Enjoy coffee and the good old analog world.

2. AUGARTEN
A wonderful park with two restaurants and a relaxed atmosphere.

3. AM NORDPOL
Hearty Bohemian food at its best. An establishment loved by the locals.

4. MRAZ & SOHN – *My favorite fine-dining restaurant* in Vienna, full of surprises and culinary entertainment.

5. HANNOVERMARKT >> PAGE 6

6. WOHNKÜCHE – Chef Andy guarantees a relaxed atmosphere and local cuisine with a modern twist. Thumbs up for this little gem!

7. ZWISCHENBRÜCKENWIRT – You'll get good value for money in this hidden-away restaurant, which serves modern local food.

8. STOMACH – A short walk from the tram stop, which is more than worth it. This venerable establishment has a great atmosphere, with a wonderful garden – and happily, good food too.

9. BEAVER BREWING – American-inspired craft beer with a local touch.

10. LEONES – Viennese ice cream at its best! Never opt for the small helping.

10. CRÉME DE LA CRÉME – Mon Dieu! It's hard to resist this wonderful pastry. A small café with coffee that's not to be missed.

11. DELI BLUEM – Vegan pioneer in Vienna which serves lunch and coffee in a beautiful atmosphere.

Join us in Vienna

COOKINVIENNA.COM

BEFORE YOU START *cooking*...

This book is designed to travel the world!

We've been hosting visitors for more than 7 years and it is thanks to our guests that we felt so well-prepared to produce this book. It's often been requested, but I've never found the time until now.

YES – now our recipes can travel with you and be a *lasting souvenir* of your trip.

No recipe is carved in stone.

So feel free to augment, reduce, add and alter them just as you like. Take my recipes as inspiration for Austrian cuisine and lifestyle, but never take them too seriously. I've tried to simplify the ingredients and recipes, so they can work anywhere in the world.

We've also tried to describe everything as precisely as possible, but perhaps you're a chef yourself and don't need detailed descriptions.

This book is dedicated to everybody who *loves to eat and travel!*

A LITTLE LEEWAY ...

All our recipes have been cooked several times and proof-checked with great care by different people. Nevertheless, due to the diverse ingredients, conversion of measurements and language differences, a few minor mistakes may possibly have crept in. If so, please believe that we did our best!

A BRIEF GLOSSARY BEFORE YOU START

butter	always *unsalted* – SEE PAGE 61 >>
fl oz	fluid ounce
g	gram
kg	kilo
ml	milliliter
pepper	We only use *fresh ground pepper.*
oz	ounces
tsp	teaspoon
tbsp	tablespoon

DELICIOUS VIENNESE EGG SPREAD

EIERAUFSTRICH * SERVES 4-6

6	6	eggs
250 g	8.8 oz	fresh curd cheese –"TOPFEN"– SEE PAGE 61 >>
100 g	3.5 oz	cream cheese, such as Philadelphia
1 tbsp	1 tbsp	mustard
1	1	small onion, chopped finely
4 tbsp	4 tbsp	pickled cucumbers, chopped finely
1 tbsp	1 tbsp	water of the pickled cucumbers
		salt, pepper
		chives, chopped

PREPARATION

- Boil the eggs for 12-15 minutes, then chill them in cold or ice water. Peel all eggs.

- Peel the whites of 2 eggs, dice them small and place in a separate bowl.

- The remaining eggs and egg yolks can be roughly chopped in a bowl.

- Mix all ingredients, except the diced egg whites, together. Once they are well blended, also add the egg whites and season the mixture well.

- Serve on white or sourdough bread, sprinkled with chopped chives.

FAMOUS POTATO SPREAD

ERDÄPFELAUFSTRICH * SERVES 4-6

500 g	18 oz	potatoes
250 g	8.8 oz	cream cheese, such as Philadelphia
100 g	3.5 oz	crème fraiche or sour cream
1	1	small onion, chopped finely
1 clove	1 clove	garlic, minced finely
		salt, pepper
¼ tbsp	¼ tbsp	caraway seeds, lightly pestled
		chopped chives to serve

- Boil the potatoes the night before in salted water and allow to cool down completely.

- Mix the cheese and crème fraiche together.

- Mash the peeled potatoes in a bowl using a press or a masher, mix with all the other ingredients and season well.

- Let the mixture sit for 30 minutes and season it again before serving on sourdough bread, sprinkled with chives.

SPICY BELL PEPPER SPREAD

ROASTED PUMPKIN SEED SPREAD

DELICIOUS VIENNESE EGG SPREAD

FAMOUS POTATO SPREAD

SPRING SPREAD

These spreads are served in every "HEURIGEN" – SEE PAGE 5 >>
They go perfectly with a glass of wine or beer.

CURD CHEESE SPREADS

TOPFENAUFSTRICHE • SERVES 4-6

BASIC INGREDIENTS

60 g	2 oz	butter, at room temperature
2 tbsp	2 tbsp	crème fraiche
250 g	8.8 oz	fresh curd cheese -"TOPFEN"- SEE PAGE 61 >>
2 tbsp	2 tbsp	onions, chopped finely
1 clove	1 clove	garlic, minced finely
		salt, pepper

+ SPICY BELL PEPPER SPREAD – LIPTAUER

2 tbsp	2 tbsp	pickled cucumbers, chopped finely
1 tbsp	1 tbsp	pickled capers, chopped
1 tbsp	1 tbsp	mustard and bell pepper powder
a pinch	a pinch	chili or spice paprika powder
¼ tsp	¼ tsp	caraway seeds, lightly pestled
		chopped chives to serve

+ SPRING SPREAD - FRÜHLINGSAUFSTRICH

4 tbsp	4 tbsp	garden radishes, diced small
2 tbsp	2 tbsp	herbs like chives, dill or parsley, chopped
1 tbsp	1 tbsp	horseradish, ground or minced

+ ROASTED PUMPKIN SEED SPREAD – KÜRBISKERNAUFSTRICH

2 tbsp	2 tbsp	roasted pumpkin seed oil – SEE PAGE 34 >>
2 tbsp	2 tbsp	roasted pumpkin seeds, coarsely crunched

- Beat the butter with crème fraiche in a bowl until creamy.
- Add the curd cheese and all the other ingredients.
  Season your spread with salt, pepper or herbs.
- Serve the spread with fresh or toasted sourdough bread.

You can also use FETA *instead of fresh curd cheese.
In that case, you should reduce the amount of additional salt.*

CREAMY CUCUMBER SALAD

RAHM-GURKENSALAT * SERVES 4

2 (1 kg)	2 (35 oz)	cucumbers
		salt
2 tbsp	2 tbsp	chopped dill
1 clove	1 clove	garlic, thinly cut or crushed
a dash	a dash	vinegar
200 g	7 oz	sour cream, or prepare a mixture of
		10 % yoghurt and crème fraiche

- Use the cucumbers peeled or unpeeled and slice them thinly into a bowl, where you mix them with ½ tsp of salt.
- Let the salted cucumbers sit for 20 minutes before gently squeezing them to get the water out.
- Season the water-free cucumbers with dill, garlic, a dash of vinegar, sour cream and salt.

TRADITIONAL CABBAGE SALAD

KRAUTSALAT * SERVES 4

800 g	21 oz	cabbage without stem
		salt
4 tbsp	4 tbsp	vinegar
6 tbsp	6 tbsp	oil
½ tsp	½ tsp	caraway seeds
a pinch	a pinch	sugar

- Quarter the cabbage and cut thinly. Knead it well with salt in a bowl and let it sit for 30 minutes.
- Squeeze out the water and season with salt, vinegar, oil, caraway seeds and a pinch of sugar.

*Caraway is the oldest spice in the world &
frequently used in Austrian dishes.
Besides its full flavor, other positive side effects
are its antibacterial and digestion-friendly properties.*

TRADITIONAL
POTATO SALAD

SPICY
BEETROOT SALAD

TRADITIONAL
CABBAGE SALAD

CREAMY
CUCUMBER SALAD

POTATO &
FIELD SALAD

SPICY BEETROOT SALAD
ROTE RÜBEN-SALAT ∗ SERVES 4-6

800 g	28 oz	beetroot
		salt
2 tbsp	2 tbsp	ground horseradish
1 tbsp	1 tbsp	apricot or raspberry jam
a pinch	a pinch	lemon zest
1-2 tbsp	1-2 tbsp	lemon juice or vinegar
½ tsp	½ tsp	cumin or caraway seeds
2 tbsp	2 tbsp	chopped dill

PREPARATION

- Boil the cleaned beetroots in salt water until they are soft. Peel the roots while still warm and slice or chop them roughly into a bowl.

- Mix with the other ingredients while they are still warm and season well, as the beetroots will absorb the spices.

- Allow to cool, season again and serve with a generous sprinkling of dill. You can easily keep this salad in the fridge for a week.

Beetroots
are a REGIONAL SUPERFOOD
– a tasty, healthy all-rounder!

TRADITIONAL POTATO SALAD

ERDÄPFELSALAT * SERVES 4-6

800 g	28 oz	waxy potatoes
1	1	small onion, thinly diced
1 tsp	1 tsp	mustard
a pinch	a pinch	salt, sugar and pepper
4 tbsp	4 tbsp	vinegar
8 tbsp	4 tbsp	oil
250 ml	8.4 fl oz	warm stock or water
		finely chopped chives

PREPARATION

- Boil the potatoes in their skins in hot water until they are soft.
- Peel and slice the potatoes while they are still warm and season them in a bowl with all ingredients. Garnish with chives.
- Serve with a schnitzel or a sandwich –

this salad goes with everything!

- If you like more greens, then serve with lamb's lettuce or field salad.

THE KEY TO MAKING
this salad is to season while the potatoes are still warm,
so that they absorb all the flavors of the seasoning.

Austrians love potatoes, and call them
"KARTOFFELN" or "ERDÄPFEL"
– which, literally translated, means "EARTH APPLES".

VIENNESE POTATO SOUP

ALT WIENER ERDÄPFELSUPPE * SERVES 4

1 tbsp	1 tbsp	dried porcini
150 g	5 oz	bacon >> or without, if you like it vegetarian
1	1	onion
2 cloves	2 cloves	garlic
600 g	21 oz	potatoes
150 g	5 oz	carrots
2 tbsp	2 tbsp	oil
½ tsp	½ tsp	caraway seeds
1 tbsp	1 tbsp	marjoram
1 liter	34 fl oz	water
		salt, pepper
2	2	bay leaves
100 g	3.5 oz	sour cream or crème fraiche
1 tbsp	1 tbsp	flour
a dash	a dash	vinegar

PREPARATION

- Soak the mushrooms in hot water in a cup.

- Separately dice bacon and peeled vegetables small: onion, garlic, potatoes and carrots, and store in separate bowls.

- Heat the oil and fry the bacon in a pot until crispy. Add onions until translucent, then the garlic and after a minute, the potatoes, carrots, caraway seeds, marjoram and soaked mushrooms. Add water and season with salt, pepper and bay leaves. Let it simmer until the potatoes are al dente.

- Stir the sour cream with flour in a mug and add 3-4 tbsp hot soup. Then mix it into the hot soup. After bringing it to the boil, turn down the heat. The soup should have thickened a bit.

- Season the soup with salt, pepper and a dash of vinegar to taste.

BEEF BROTH

RINDSUPPE • SERVES 6

1 tbsp	1 tbsp	oil
2	2	onions
500 g	18 oz	beef for boiling
		(brisket, chuck or shoulder roast)
300 g	10 oz	beef bones
2 cloves	2 cloves	garlic, peeled
3	3	carrots, peeled
4	4	sticks of celery
½	½	leek
3	3	parsley stalks
10	10	peppercorns
5	5	allspice berries
		salt

PREPARATION

- Cut the onions, together with their skins, in half and fry them in oil on the cut surface in a large pot, until dark brown.

- Add the beef with all other ingredients and 2.5 liters / 84 fl oz of cold water and 1-2 tsp salt.

- Bring it **to the boil** once and let it simmer with no lid for 1.5 - 2 hours. While simmering, remove the foam on top.

- Strain the soup through a very fine sieve or use a dish towel in the sieve, to get a very clear soup. The clearer the soup, the longer it will keep in the fridge.

- Season the soup with salt and serve with thin soup noodles, SLICED PANCAKES or SEMOLINA DUMPLINGS >> PAGE 32.

BEEF BROTH *is the most* traditional soup *&
is found on every restaurant menu.
In a traditional Austrian menu,
a beef broth would be the starter
followed by the main dish and dessert.*

SEMOLINA DUMPLINGS

GRIESNOCKERL * SERVES 4

30 g	1 oz	butter, at room temperature
80 g	2.8 oz	semolina
1	1	egg
		salt, grated nutmeg

- Beat the butter for 2 minutes, before adding semolina, egg, a pinch of salt and nutmeg.
- Let the dough sit in the fridge for at least 30 minutes.
- Heat up a pot of salted water.
- Use your wet hands or 2 wet teaspoons to shape small, long dumplings, which are cooked in the simmering water until they float on the top for 5-10 minutes.
- Serve the dumplings with a VEGETABLE or BEEF BROTH >> PAGE 31.

SLICED PANCAKE

FRITTATEN * SERVES 4

100 g	3.5 oz	cake flour
a pinch	a pinch	salt
1	1	egg
250 ml	8.4 fl oz	milk
		butter

- Mix flour and salt in a bowl before adding the egg and milk. Whisk well and let the batter sit for 30 minutes.
- Heat up a pan, take it off the stove and melt 1 tsp of butter. Still holding the pan in your hands, add 1 ladle of dough to one side and let it slowly cover the rest of the pan. It should be thin, like a crepe.
- Let it bake slightly brown before turning it over onto the other side. Let it bake for another minute before putting it on a plate.
- Once the pancakes have cooled down a little bit, roll the pancake into a sausage shape, cut it into thin strips and serve with VEGETABLE or BEEF BROTH >> PAGE 31.

SLICED PANCAKE

SEMOLINA DUMPLINGS

THIS IS AUSTRIAN *soul food* !

SEXY SQUASH SOUP

SEXY KÜRBISCREMESUPPE * SERVES 4

1	1	onion
2 pieces	2 pieces	garlic
2 tbsp	2 tbsp	oil
400 g	14 oz	squash, such as Hokkaido* or butternut
1-2	1-2	carrots
		chili – if you like it hot
1 tbsp	1 tbsp	ginger, grated or chopped
		salt, pepper
½ tsp	½ tsp	all-spice
0.7 liter	24 fl oz	water
zest of ½	zest of ½	lemon
100 g	3 oz	crème fraiche or coconut cream
		Austrian roasted pumpkin seed oil

- Dice onion and garlic.
- Coarsely chop the washed, seed-free squash and peeled carrots.
- Heat up a pot with oil and roast onions until translucent, then add the garlic and fry for one minute.
- Add squash and carrots to the pot and roast them together with chili, ginger, salt, pepper and all-spice for one minute.
- Add water and lemon zest and let it boil until the squash is soft.
- Purée with a blender, and finally season the soup with crème fraiche or coconut cream and spices.
- Serve the soup with a few dashes of pumpkin seed oil.

* Hokkaido doesn't need to be peeled.
All other varieties must be peeled first.

Austrian roasted pumpkin seed oil
is dark like fuel. It tastes very nutty and
is intensive in flavor.

Roasted pumpkin seed oil
makes a great gift for friends and family!

BROWN BREAD
DUMPLINGS

PRETZEL
DUMPLINGS

CLASSIC BREAD
DUMPLINGS

BREAD DUMPLINGS OR "NAPKIN ROLLS"
SERVIETTENSCHNITTEN • SERVES 4

BROWN BREAD DUMPLINGS - SCHWARZBROTKNÖDEL

230 g	8 oz	stale brown bread, diced small
70 g	2.5 oz	stale white sandwich bread, diced small
230 ml	7.8 fl oz	milk
1	1	onion
2 tbsp	2 tbsp	butter
3	3	eggs
2 tbsp	2 tbsp	parsley, chopped
¾ tsp	¾ tsp	salt
a pinch	a pinch	pepper, nutmeg

CLASSIC BREAD DUMPLINGS - SERVIETTENSCHNITTEN

500 g	18 oz	stale white sandwich bread without crust, diced small
120 ml	4 fl oz	milk
1	1	onion
2 tbsp	2 tbsp	butter
2	2	eggs
2 tbsp	2 tbsp	parsley, chopped
¾ tsp	¾ tsp	salt
a pinch	a pinch	pepper, nutmeg

- Soak the bread in milk in a bowl for 10 minutes.
- Dice the onion small and fry in a pan with butter until translucent.
- Add onions, eggs, parsley, salt, pepper and nutmeg to the bread and mix well.
- Shape a roll on a piece of clingfilm, wrap it and close it well at both ends. Then wrap it in a dish towel or in tinfoil and close the ends well, using a string if necessary.
- Allow to simmer in water for about 30 minutes. Unwrap the dumpling and slice it. Eat the dumplings right away or fry with butter in a pan.
- Serve the dumplings with GOULASH >> PAGE 55, RED PAPRIKA CHICKEN STEW >> PAGE 59 or CREAMY MUSHROOMS >> PAGE 45.

PRETZEL DUMPLINGS

BREZENKNÖDEL * SERVES 4

230 g	8 oz	pretzels, roughly diced
100 ml	3.2 fl oz	milk
60 g	2 oz	butter
2	2	eggs
¾ tsp	¾ tsp	salt
a pinch	a pinch	pepper, nutmeg

- Soak the pretzels in milk in a bowl for 10 minutes.
- Beat the butter with egg yolks in a bowl.
  Whisk the egg whites in a separate bowl.
- Carefully mix all ingredients and season with spices.
- Shape a roll on a piece of clingfilm, wrap it and close it well at both ends. Then wrap it in a napkin, dish towel or tinfoil and close the ends well, using a string if necessary.
- Allow to simmer in water for about 30 minutes. Unwrap the dumpling and slice it. Eat the dumplings right away or fry with butter in a pan.

THE KINGS OF AUSTRIAN CUISINE

Dumplings – Knödel

DUMPLINGS play a very important role in Austrian cuisine and every region has different recipes. It is used as a generic term and they can have different sizes, shapes, ingredients and very diverse consistencies and tastes. We eat them in soups, as a main or side dish and as a sweet dish.

Dumplings can be traced back to very ancient times and have their roots in the Alpine region. The word "KNÖDEL" comes from the Latin "nodus" and means "KNOT".

The "KAISER ROLL" or "SEMMEL", which is the most traditional bun and is even named after the Emperor ("Kaiser") in English, tastes crispy and fluffy once it's fresh, but dull when it gets dry the next day: so they had to invent a recipe using the old bread. Thus, "SERVIETTEN SCHNITTE" or "SEMMELKNÖDEL" are the most popular dumplings in Vienna and are based on Kaiser Rolls.

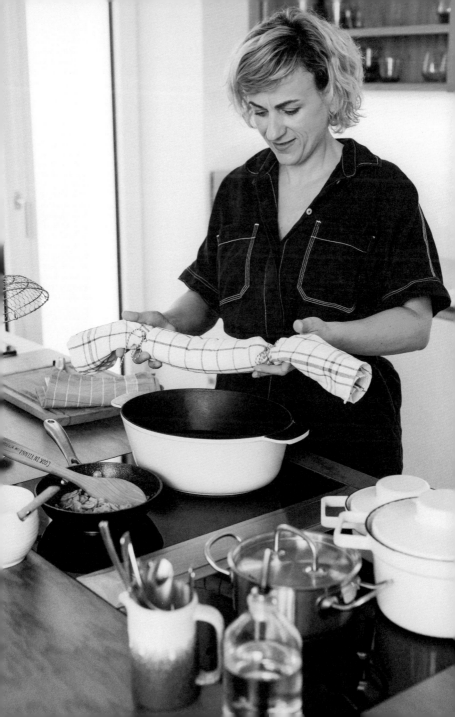

CRISPY POTATO & ROOT VEGGIE FRITTERS WITH GARLIC DIP

ERDÄPFEL- UND GEMÜSEPUFFER MIT KNOBLAUCHSAUCE ∗ SERVES 4

CLASSIC

500 g	18 oz	potatoes
¾ tsp	¾ tsp	salt
a pinch	a pinch	nutmeg
2 tbsp	2 tbsp	all-purpose flour
		oil

FANCY

300 g	10.6 oz	potatoes
200 g	7.0 oz	parsnips or carrots or beetroots
¾ tsp	¾ tsp	salt
2 tbsp	2 tbsp	fresh herbs like parsley, dill and rosemary, cut coarsely
2 tbsp	2 tbsp	all-purpose flour
		oil

FOR THE GARLIC DIP

200 g	7.0 oz	sour cream **OR**
150 g	5.3 oz	crème fraiche, stirred with 3 tbsp water
1-2 cloves	1-2 cloves	garlic, minced
zest of ½	zest of ½	lemon
a pinch	a pinch	salt, pepper and sugar
1 tbsp	1 tbsp	chives, chopped

- Peel the potatoes or root vegetables and grate them with a "Rösti grater" or potato grater in separate bowls and let it sit for 15 minutes.
- Squeeze the water out of the potatoes by hand and place in a new bowl or add to the other grated root vegetables.
- IMPORTANT: Pour the left-over water away and also add the potato starch remaining in the bottom of the bowl to the potatoes.
- Now mix in all the other ingredients and let it sit for another 5 minutes. The mixture should have a thick consistency.
- Heat some oil in a pan and use a fork to flatten approximately 1 tbsp of the mixture in sizzling oil to make each fritter. Slowly fry the fritters until they are crispy on both sides.
- FOR THE GARLIC DIP: Mix all the ingredients together and season well.
- Enjoy the crispy root veggies with the dip and a fresh lettuce salad.

A perfect
side dish to
BEEF GOULASH
>> PAGE 55 or
CHICKEN STEW
>> PAGE 59.

Don't forget to
buy your
SPAETZLI GRATER
in Vienna as a
SOUVENIR.

The Austrian version of MACARONI CHEESE
*– immensely popular with young and old alike!
Enjoy them at home or in an Alpine hut on a skiing trip.
No Austrian ever says no to these – they always go down well!*

MAGIC SPAETZLI

SPÄTZLE, KÄSESPÄTZLE, EIERSPÄTZLE * SERVES 4

BASIC BATTER

350 g	12.3 oz	all-purpose flour
½ tsp	½ tsp	salt
4	4	eggs
125 ml	4.2 fl oz	milk
		butter and salt for seasoning

PIMP THEM WITH CHEESE			PIMP THEM WITH EGGS	
	oil for frying		4	eggs
2	onions, sliced thinly			salt, pepper
2 tbsp	butter		3 tbsp	butter
5 tbsp	grated cheese		1 tbsp	chives, chopped
	salt, pepper			

- FOR THE BASIC BATTER: Mix flour with salt in a larger bowl. Using a wooden spoon, fold in the other ingredients to make a thick, but smooth batter. Let it sit for 10 minutes.

- Bring a large pot of salted water to the boil and put the Spaetzli grater on top. Now lower the temperature to medium heat. Make sure that there is no direct contact between water and grater.

- Start to work the batter through the grater while continuously stirring with a wooden spoon to prevent the Spaetzli from sticking together or on the bottom.

- Let the Spaetzli simmer, until they are floating on top. Now you can rinse them well in a strainer with hot water. Pour away the water from the pot, put the Spaetzli back in the pot and season with butter, a dash of water and salt.

- FOR CRISPY CHEESE SPAETZLI: Heat oil in a pot and first fry the onions until crispy.

- Preheat the oven to 220 °C.

- Heat the Spaetzli with butter in an ovenproof pan or receptacle, mix them with 2/3 of the cheese and sprinkle the remainder on top. Bake until crispy and golden-brown on top. Serve with crispy onions on top and lettuce salad.

- FOR TRADITIONAL EGG SPAETZLI: Whisk the eggs well together in a bowl and season with ½ tsp of salt.

- First heat the Spaetzli with butter in a pan and then stir in the eggs. Season with salt, pepper and a sprinkling of chives on top. Serve with lettuce salad.

CREAMY MUSHROOMS WITH BREAD DUMPLINGS

SCHWAMMERLSAUCE MIT SERVIETTENSCHNITTEN * SERVES 4

1	1	onion
4 tbsp	4 tbsp	butter
800 g	28 oz	mushrooms
1 clove	1 clove	garlic
		salt, pepper
125 ml	4.2 fl oz	white wine or water
6 tbsp	6 tbsp	crème fraiche
2 tbsp	2 tbsp	all-purpose flour
zest of ½	zest of ½	lemon
3 tbsp	3 tbsp	chopped parsley

PREPARATION

- Dice the peeled onion small and fry with butter in a pan until translucent.
- Slice the mushrooms and fry them on a low heat together with chopped garlic in the pan. Season with salt and pepper.
- Whisk the wine with the crème fraiche and flour in a separate mug. Once the mushrooms have been fried slightly brown, add the crème and turn up the heat so that it thickens. Once the mixture is thick and creamy, turn down the heat.
- Season the mushrooms with the lemon zest, salt, pepper and half of the parsley.
- Serve with the BREAD DUMPLINGS >> PAGE 37 and the remaining parsley on top.

Austrians love chantarelle!
During chantarelle season you will find it on every menu.

This sauce also *goes well with* roasted red meat or pasta.

SPINACH DUMPLINGS WITH CARAMELIZED BUTTER

SPINATKNÖDEL MIT BRAUNER BUTTER * SERVES 4

500 g	17.6 oz	fresh spinach **OR**
100 g	3.5 oz	frozen spinach
1	1	onion, diced small
1 tbsp	1 tbsp	butter
2 cloves	2 cloves	garlic, diced small
350 g	12.3 oz	white sandwich bread
125 ml	4.2 fl oz	milk
2	2	eggs
½ tsp	½ tsp	salt
a pinch	a pinch	nutmeg
1 tbsp	1 tbsp	parsley, chopped
3 tbsp	3 tbsp	a mature cheese such as mountain, cheddar or farm cheese, grated
2 tbsp	2 tbsp	all-purpose flour
5 tbsp	5 tbsp	butter
a pinch	a pinch	salt
		for serving mature cheese, grated

PIMP THE DUMPLING with a piece of feta cheese in the middle

- Blanch the fresh spinach briefly in salty water or defrost the frozen spinach. Then rinse it well before cutting it into fine pieces.
- Roast the onions and garlic with butter in a pan until translucent.
- Dice the bread small and mix it well with all ingredients in a bowl. Let it sit for 15 minutes.
- IMPORTANT: When you prepare dumplings, always start with a small "test dumpling" to check if the ingredients stick together well. If not, add 1 tbsp flour and let it sit again.
- Bring a large pot of salted water to the boil. Roll 8-12 dumplings with wet hands and press them well together.
- Allow to simmer in the water with a lid on top.
- FOR THE CARAMELIZED BUTTER: Put the butter in a pan and heat it slowly on a low to medium temperature until the butter is golden-brown. Never leave the pan unattended. Add a pinch of salt.
- Take out the warm dumplings with a slotted spoon to the warm butter. Serve them with warm butter, with cheese sprinkled on top and a lettuce salad.

TRADITIONAL POTATO GOULASH
ERDÄPFELGULASCH * SERVES 4

800 g	28 oz	potatoes
2	2	carrots
1	1	red pepper
300 g	10 oz	onions
3 clove	3 clove	garlic
4 tbsp	4 tbsp	oil
2 tbsp	2 tbsp	tomato purée
1 tsp	1 tsp	dried marjoram
1-2 tbsp	1-2 tbsp	paprika powder
1 tsp	1 tsp	caraway seeds, lightly pestled
a pinch	a pinch	chili powder - if desired
1 tsp	1 tsp	vinegar
		salt
1 tbsp	1 tbsp	flour

PIMP THE GOULASH with chunks of Wiener sausages

- Peel the potatoes and carrots and chop coarsely.
  Get rid of the seeds from the bell pepper and dice small.

- Dice the peeled onions and garlic separately.

- Heat the oil in a pot and slowly fry the onions until slightly brown,
  adding the garlic for another minute.

- Roast the tomato purée with the onions and, finally,
  quickly add all the spices.

- Deglaze with vinegar and 800 ml / 27 fl oz water.

- Add 1 tsp salt, bring to the boil and allow to simmer until the
  potatoes are soft. Season to taste and add the sausages for another
  5 minutes.

- If you'd like a thicker sauce, stir flour into 3 tbsp water in cup and
  add it to the goulash. Bring to boil once and then season well
  with salt and vinegar.

This is a traditional family weekday dish &
is loved by kids, who fight for the sausage.
In my family, we enjoyed it with pasta & a salad as side dish.

CARAMELIZED CABBAGE WITH NOODLES

KRAUTFLECKERL • SERVES 4

300 g	10 oz	Fleckerl or small pasta squares
1 large	1 large	onion
8 tbsp	8 tbsp	oil
100 g	4 oz	bacon, diced, if desired
4 tbsp	4 tbsp	granulated sugar
600 g	21 oz	white cabbage
3 tbsp	3 tbsp	water
½ tsp	½ tsp	caraway seeds, coarsely pestled
		salt, pepper
a dash	a dash	vinegar
2 tbsp	2 tbsp	crème fraiche or sour cream
2 tbsp	2 tbsp	chives, chopped

- Boil the pasta in enough hot salt water until it's al dente. Rinse with cold water in a strainer.

- Finely dice the onion and fry with bacon in oil until the onion is slightly brown. Then add the sugar and roast it dark brown.

- Cut the cabbage leaves into pieces approximately the same size as the pasta and add it, together with the water, to the onions.

- Season with caraway seeds, salt, pepper and a dash of vinegar.

- Now fry the cabbage till soft. Then add the pasta, mix it well with the cabbage and season to taste.

- Finally, add crème fraiche and serve with chives.

FLECKERL is a small square-shaped Austrian pasta, which is always served as a main dish with cabbage as well as with meat, sausage or bacon.

Instead, you can use a small Italian pasta like orecchiette.

WIENER SCHNITZEL

WIENER SCHNITZEL * SERVES 4

800 g	28 oz	veal top round, trimmed well, cut into 4 cutlets and butterflied
		salt
		flour
2	2	eggs
		breadcrumbs
		oil or butter oil for frying

Slice of lemon and cranberry jam for serving

- Make one small, shallow cut on each side of each cutlet. This helps to prevent them rolling up.
- Cover the cutlets individually with clingfilm and pound each one with a meat mallet until very thin - approx. 6 mm /0.2 inches.
- Set out three soup plates or larger kitchen bowls, in which you place the ingredients in the following order: flour, beaten eggs with a pinch of salt and breadcrumbs.
- Heat up enough oil, lard or butter oil for frying in a large pan.
- You can now start on the Schnitzel. Work fast and follow the GOLDEN RULES!
- Season the meat with salt and cover it with flour. Before coating it with egg, dust off the excess flour by gently shaking the meat.
- Use your hands and a fork to pull the meat through the beaten eggs.
- Allow the excess egg to drip off a little before finally putting the meat into the breadcrumbs. Never use your hands to fix the breadcrumb coating.
- Now fry the Schnitzel golden-brown on both sides.
- Serve with **POTATO SALAD** >>PAGE 27 or boiled potatoes.

Real WIENER SCHNITZEL *must always be made of veal* !
*You can also find schnitzel made from pork, chicken or turkey –
only then it's "not allowed" to be called WIENER Schnitzel,
but just Schnitzel!*

- Work fast and never let it sit in one of the ingredients too long.

- Never use your hands to fix the breadcrumb coating on the Schnitzel.

- After covering it in the breadcrumbs, you should fry the Schnitzel immediately.

- Use enough oil for the Schnitzel to be able to float and shake the pan constantly while frying.

- Regulate the heat well!

Paprika powder
is a common feature of
AUSTRIAN & HUNGARIAN CUISINE:
the goulash is the same – but different!

The sauce
IS THE KEY!

BEEF GOULASH

RINDSGULASCH * SERVES 4

800 g	28 oz	onions
3 gloves	3 gloves	garlic
		oil
3-4 tbsp	3-4 tbsp	paprika powder
a pinch	a pinch	chili - if desired
1 tsp	1 tsp	marjoram
½ tsp	½ tsp	caraway seeds
2 tbsp	2 tbsp	tomato purée
a dash	a dash	vinegar
		salt
2	2	bay leaves
800 g	28 oz	stewing beef, cut into 3 cm chunks

> THIS IS A PERFECT RECIPE FOR YOUR SLOW-COOKER!

- Peel onions and garlic and dice small separately.
- Heat up 3-4 tbsp of oil in a pot and fry the onions slowly until they are slightly brown. Add garlic and fry with the paprika powder, chili, marjoram, caraway seeds and tomato purée for 2 minutes.
- Deglaze with vinegar and ½ liter / 17 fl oz of water. Season with salt and allow to simmer for 20 minutes.
- Mix the onions to a sauce with a hand blender or leave the pot to simmer with the meat until the onions have dissolved.
- Add bay leaves and meat to the sauce. Cover the pot with a lid.
- Put the pot on or (if ovenproof) in the oven on a low to medium heat. The meat should be covered by the sauce. If you need more liquid, just add a little water.
- In total it will take around 1.5 - 2.5 hours until the meat is soft.
- Season with salt, vinegar or chili and serve with BREAD DUMPLINGS >> PAGE 37 or SPAETZLI >> PAGE 43 and a CABBAGE >> PAGE 24 or CUCUMBER SALAD >> PAGE 24 as side dish.

Of course, there is one good reason for eating GOULASH in a restaurant – not having to chop lots of onions!

You should use the same amount of onions as meat, so just imagine cooking masses of goulash for your extended family and friends...

JUICY BEEF ROLLS

GEFÜLLTE RINDSROULADE * SERVES 4

4	4	beef cutlets (à 170 g / 6 oz)
		salt, pepper, mustard
8-12	8-12	bacon slices
3	3	carrots, peeled, cut into sticks
2-3	2-3	pickled cucumbers, cut into sticks
1 tbsp	1 tbsp	caper berries
		oil
2	2	onions
2 gloves	2 gloves	garlic
½	½	stick of celery or ½ knob of celeriac, peeled - if necessary - and roughly chopped
3 tbsp	3 tbsp	tomato purée
1 tbsp	1 tbsp	fresh thyme
1/2 l	17 fl oz	red wine - replace with some water if desired
1	1	bay leaf
1-2 tbsp	1-2 tbsp	crème fraiche

- Lightly pound the meat with a meat mallet, sprinkle salt and pepper on both sides. Then spread a little mustard on 1 side only.

- Start placing the bacon on the schnitzel and place carrots, cucumber and caper berries on the thinner edge of the beef. Roll it up tightly and fix it with a toothpick.

- Heat some oil in an ovenproof pan and fry the meat lightly on all sides. Put it aside.

- Fry onions in the same pan. Then add garlic and the remaining carrots, roughly cut celery or celeriac.

- Add the tomato purée and cook it with the thyme for 2-3 minutes.

- Deglaze with ½ liter / 17 fl oz of wine, of water or a mixture of wine and water. Season with bay leaf, salt and pepper.

- Add the beef rolls, cover with a lid and put in the oven at 140 °C / 290 F for 1.5 hours.

- Take the pan out of the oven, set the beef rolls and bay leaf aside and blend the vegetables with a hand blender. Add the crème fraiche and season with salt and pepper.

- Serve the beef rolls with sauce, boiled or mashed potatoes and CABBAGE SALAD >> PAGE 24.

RED PAPRIKA CHICKEN STEW

PAPRIKAHUHN • SERVES 4

800 g	28 oz	chicken, with or without skin
		oil
		salt, pepper
2	2	onions, diced small
2 gloves	2 gloves	garlic, diced small
4	4	red paprika, roughly chopped
2 tbsp	2 tbsp	tomato purée
0.75 l	25 fl oz	water
4 tbsp	4 tbsp	crème fraiche
1-2 tbsp	1-2 tbsp	paprika powder
		chili - if desired
1 tsp	1 tsp	marjoram
2	2	bay leaves
a dash	a dash	vinegar
		chopped chives for serving

PREPARATION

- Cut the chicken into small pieces and season with salt and pepper.
- Heat 3 tbsp oil in a pan and fry the pieces until golden-brown on each side. Put them on an extra plate.
- If necessary, add 1-2 tbsp oil and first fry the onion until slightly brown, then add the garlic and red paprika.
- Add the tomato purée and cook for another 2 minutes. Add paprika powder, chili if desired, marjoram and bay leaves.
- Deglaze with a dash of vinegar and water. Take out the bay leaves and mix the sauce with a hand blender.
- Add the chicken and let it simmer again for 15-20 minutes. Add crème fraiche and season with salt and pepper to taste.
- Serve it with SPAETZLI >> PAGE 43, noodles or DUMPLINGS >> PAGE 37 and chives.

THE *essentials* ON SWEET AUSTRIAN DISHES

Austrian pastries aren't as delicate or as fragile as the French variety, but have a full, seasonal flavor. Sweet dishes are also often served as a main dish, especially on Fridays.

The magic white powder: Flour - MEHL

Austrian cuisine is based on flour and we mostly use wheat flour for baking, but also use rye flour and other varieties for making bread. When you visit an Austrian supermarket, you'll find a big selection of different qualities and variations of flour, which shows how important it is in our cuisine. If you don't find such a wide range of different qualities in your supermarket, don't worry! Just get an all-purpose or baking flour.

We even call our sweet dishes "MEHLSPEISEN" – which, literally translated, means "FLOUR DISHES". This category is huge in Austrian cuisine and includes not only sweet main dishes which we eat for lunch, but also cakes or strudel. Yes, if you have a sweet tooth, you'll feel you're in heaven in Austria!

Sugar - ZUCKER

We mainly use two different kinds of sugar: CONFECTIONER'S and GRANULATED SUGAR.

Vanilla Sugar - VANILLEZUCKER

Vanilla is exquisite, and it's essential in Austrian pastries. We mostly use the pod or sugar seasoned with it – so I recommend that you first prepare some vanilla sugar before baking my recipes.

| 1 | 1 | vanilla pod |
| 400 g | 14 oz | granulated or confectioner's sugar |

- Slice the vanilla pod, take out the seeds and put both into a pint jar. Cover them with sugar and shake well.

- Leave it for a few days, shaking the jar occasionally, before using the sugar. Feel free to replace the sugar, since the vanilla pod has a lot of flavor.

Breadcrumbs - SEMMELBRÖSEL

Breadcrumbs are basically just a recycled product of Kaiser rolls or white bread and are often used in our sweet dishes.

You'll find several brands of "SEMMELBRÖSEL" in every supermarket or bakery. The dried breadcrumbs taste simply dull and are crying out for... butter – which turns them into a nutty, tasty ingredient in dumplings, strudel, etc.

Curd cheese - TOPFEN

Austrians love dairy products. In particular, curd cheese or quark ("TOPFEN") is used for several sweet dishes, strudel, cakes and spreads. I've learnt from my visiting guests that a similar cheese is available under the name "FARMER'S CHEESE" in America.

Butter

Austrian butter is full of flavor and always sweet, **never salted**. In the past, people also used lard or butter oil, but nowadays butter is the most common fat used in baking. We also use oil for cooking, but butter is always the main ingredient for seasoning.

Scales

Measuring cups don't exist in Austria and we only use scales for baking. **Please don't be scared off** by my recipes – invest in a pair of kitchen scales which will make baking easier and perhaps even **more successful**.

SACHER CAKE

SACHER TORTE * SERVES 12

140 g	5 oz	plain chocolate
140 g	5 oz	unsalted butter
2 tbsp	2 tbsp	confectioner's sugar
½ tsp	½ tsp	vanilla extract or 1 tbsp vanilla sugar
5	5	eggs
85 g	3 oz	granulated sugar
140 g	5 oz	cake flour

1 tbsp butter and flour to grease the cake pan

FOR THE FILLING AND GLAZE

230 g	8 oz	apricot jam
140 g	5 oz	plain chocolate
140 g	5 oz	unsalted butter, softened

Whipped cream to garnish

USE ALL INGREDIENTS AT ROOM TEMPERATURE

PREPARATION

- Preheat the oven to 180 °C/ 355 °F. Grease a deep 9-inch/23-cm round cake pan with butter and dust with flour.

- PREPARE THE CAKE MIX: Melt pieces of chocolate in a pan over another pan containing water simmering **on a gentle heat.** When it is melted completely, allow to cool a little.

- **Beat the butter with confectioner's sugar** and **vanilla sugar** in a larger bowl for about 3 minutes.

- **Add one egg yolk at time**, mixing well after adding each yolk. Slowly add melted, tepid chocolate while mixing.

- **In another bowl**, whisk the egg whites for about 2 minutes, until slightly foamy. Slowly add granulated sugar and whisk until the egg whites can hold a soft peak.

- **Start mixing one third of the egg whites** into the egg yolk and chocolate mixture with a spatula or wooden spoon. Then gently fold in the rest of the egg whites.

- **Fold in the flour**, using a sieve to evenly distribute it over the top of the batter while you fold it in.

- **Pour the mixture** into the greased pan and level the surface evenly with a spoon.
- **Bake for about 40-45 minutes**, or until the cake springs back when lightly pressed with a finger. Allow to cool for 20 minutes before removing from the pan. Turn it upside down so that the perfectly flat base becomes the new, even top of the cake.
- Carefully cut the cake in half horizontally using a long, serrated knife.
- FOR THE TOPPING: Heat the apricot jam in a pan and spread one third over the bottom layer and place the other layer on top.
- Sieve the remaining jam on top of the cake and spread it all over the top and sides of the cake. Leave to sit for 2 hours.
- Melt pieces of chocolate and butter in a pan over another pan containing water simmering **on a gentle heat**. Remove from the heat when just melted and stir until smooth.
- Coat the cake on the baking grid or over a baking sheet using an angled palette knife.
- After 5-10 minutes, cut the bottom of the cake and transfer to a cake plate. Allow to cool and store at around 18 °C / 62 F.
- Serve with a generous dollop of whipped cream.

Whole pages are filled with the history of this cake, which nowadays is a traditional cake baked at home and enjoyed in restaurants.

The original recipe was devised in the mid-19th century after MILK CHOCOLATE *was invented, which made a chocolate glazing possible. Before that, chocolate was not creamy and quick-melting as we know it today, but crumbly and no use for making a chocolate glaze.*

THE SACHER CAKE
is named after the inventor of the recipe, Mr. Franz Sacher, who was a chef and the owner of a deli. The recipe was already first published in a cookbook in 1912 and is no secret at all.

Mr. Sacher was a well-known and successful chef who cooked for several aristocrats.

LINZER CAKE

LINZER TORTE ∗ SERVES 12

125 g	4.5 oz	unsalted butter
125 g	4.5 oz	confectioner's sugar, sifted
zest of 1	zest of 1	lemon
125 g	4.5 oz	ground almonds
1/2 tsp	1/2 tsp	vanilla seeds or extract
a pinch	a pinch	salt, cinnamon and clove powder
115 g	4 oz	cake flour
1 tsp	1 tsp	baking powder
2	2	egg yolks
200 g	7 oz	redcurrant jam

USE ALL INGREDIENTS AT ROOM TEMPERATURE

- Mix butter and sifted sugar in a bowl.
- Add lemon zest, ground almonds, vanilla seeds, spices, sifted flour and baking powder.
- Add egg yolks and quickly knead all ingredients to a dough.
- Wrap the dough in clingfilm and leave it sitting in the fridge for 30 minutes.
- Preheat the oven to 180 °C / 355 °F. Grease a 9-inch / 23-cm cake pan.
- Cut one third of the dough and return it to the fridge.
- Roll out two thirds of the dough evenly between two layers of clingfilm to reach a size of 10 inches / 25 cm – that is, 1 inch / 2 cm larger than the cake pan.
- Put the dough in the cake pan with the help of the clingfilm and spread redcurrant jam evenly over it.
- Roll out the remaining third of the dough in 0.4 inch / 1 cm dough strips and shape into a lattice on top of the redcurrant jam
- Bake for 20-25 minutes until the jam bubbles.
- Allow the Linzer Torte to cool for at least 1 hour – or better still, for 1 day – before removing from the cake pan.

This recipe is named after the city of LINZ, which is the capital of the region called "UPPER AUSTRIA" and is located 200 km (124 miles) from Vienna.

TRADITIONAL AUSTRIAN APPLE STRUDEL

APFELSTRUDEL * SERVES 8

FOR THE DOUGH

200 g	7 oz	cake flour
a pinch	a pinch	salt
2 tbsp	2 tbsp	vegetable oil
1/8 l	4 fl oz	tepid water
		oil for coating
		tablecloth

FOR THE FILLING

60 g	2 oz	butter
150 g	5 oz	breadcrumbs
6-8	6-8	sour apples, peeled and without pips
4 tbsp	4 tbsp	raisins, soaked in rum or water for 30 minutes or overnight
65 g	2 oz	granulated sugar
1 tbsp	1 tbsp	vanilla sugar – SEE PAGE 60 >> or a dash of vanilla extract
1 tbsp	1 tbsp	cinnamon
		flour for preparation
200 ml	7 fl oz	sour cream or some melted butter
		crushed walnuts - optional
60 g	2 oz	melted butter for coating

Whipped cream to garnish

Flour glossary

AUSTRIA - TYPE 700
GERMANY - TYPE 550
AMERICA - CAKE FLOUR
ITALY - TYPE 00

- START WITH THE DOUGH! Mix flour and salt in a bowl and start slowly adding oil and tepid water with a spoon.

- Once the dough gets less sticky, start kneading it on the working surface until it becomes smooth and even. The texture should be silky, moist and not sticky at the end of the process.

- Slam the dough on the working surface a couple of times, then shape it into a ball and coat it with oil. Put clingfilm over the dough and leave it sitting in the fridge for 30 minutes or more.

- Heat the oven to 200 °C/ 400 °F. Prepare a baking tray with baking parchment.

- FOR THE FILLING: Melt butter in a pan and slowly roast the bread-crumbs in it until golden brown. Never leave them unattended as they can burn very fast.

- Cut the peeled apples into smaller pieces. Mix the apples with raisins, sugar and spices thoroughly in a bowl.

- Spread flour generously on a tablecloth. Place the dough in the middle and dust it well with flour. Roll it out evenly with a rolling pin or bottle.

- NOW START WORKING WITH CONFIDENCE! Use the back of your hand to stretch the dough evenly – as you may have seen your pizza baker doing – and very thinly, until you can read a newspaper through it.

- Pile layers on top of the dough in the following order: sour cream or melted butter, then the breadcrumbs, crushed walnuts and apples. **Leave an empty area of 3 fingers' width around the edges.**

- **Close the dough by folding it inwards on 3 sides**, but not on the side opposite to where you are standing.

- Then roll it tightly towards the open side, using the table cloth. Use the tablecloth like a little strudel hammock to put the strudel into the baking tray.

- Now coat the strudel with melted butter and coat the dough underneath the closing dough as well. Bake for 30-40 minutes.

- Serve warm or cold with whipped cream.

My guests call me "the Queen of the Strudel"

This cake reminds me of my childhood!

**Every Saturday evening, we baked a cake together which
we enjoyed for breakfast on Sunday. For a very long time,
a piece of this fresh cake with a glass of cold milk was the
best meal I could imagine.**

MARBLED RING CAKE
MARMORGUGELHUPF * SERVES 12

		butter and flour for the cake pan
300 g	10 oz	unsalted butter
zest of 1	zest of 1	lemon
170 g	5.5 oz	confectioner's sugar
1 tsp	1 tsp	vanilla pods or a dash of vanilla extract
a pinch	a pinch	salt
3	3	eggs
4	4	egg yolks
4	4	egg whites
120 g	4 oz	granulated sugar
240 g	8.5 oz	cake flour, sifted
½ tsp	½ tsp	baking powder
2 tbsp	2 tbsp	cocoa powder
6 tbsp	6 tbsp	milk

USE ALL INGREDIENTS AT ROOM TEMPERATURE

PREPARATION

- Pre-heat the oven up to 180°C / 365 F.
- Grease and flour the cake pan. Mix the flour with baking powder.
- Whisk butter together with lemon zest, confectioner's sugar and vanilla pods and salt in a bowl until light and creamy.
- Add one egg or yolk at a time, mixing well after adding each one. In total, 3 eggs and 4 egg yolks.
- Beat the 4 egg whites in a bowl for 2 minutes. Slowly add the granulated sugar.
- Now, carefully combine the egg white with yolk mixture and flour with baking powder.
- Divide the mixture between 2 bowls.
- Stir cocoa powder and milk in one of the bowls.
- NOW FILL THE PAN: Take 2 spoons and use them to alternately put dollops of chocolate and vanilla dough mix into the pan.
- Take a skewer or fork and swirl it around the mixture in the tin a few times to create a marbled effect.
- Bake the cake for 50-60 minutes, until a skewer inserted into the center comes out clean.

KAISERSCHMARRN AND APPLESAUCE

KAISERSCHMARRN MIT APFELMUS * SERVES 4

6	6	eggs
60 g	2 oz	granulated sugar
zest of 1	zest of 1	lemon
		vanilla sugar
a pinch	a pinch	salt
60 g	2 oz	cake flour, sifted
60 g	2 oz	unsalted butter for baking
2 tbsp	2 tbsp	raisins soaked in rum
		confectioner's sugar
30 g	1 oz	granulated sugar
1 small	1 small	cinnamon stick
3 pieces	3 pieces	clove
500 g	18 oz	apples, peeled and without pips
		juice of half lemon

- FOR THE APPLESAUCE: Heat a small cup (200 ml / 1 fl oz) of water, sugar, cinnamon and cloves in a small kettle for 10 minutes. Remove all spices.

- Quarter the apples and add to the water with the lemon juice and boil until soft. Purée the apples in a blender, if desired and serve warm or cold.

- FOR THE KAISERSCHMARRN: Heat the oven to 200 °C /375 °C.

- Whisk the egg whites with a pinch of salt for 2 minutes. Slowly add the granulated sugar until the mixture can hold a soft peak.

- In a separate bowl, whisk egg yolk, lemon zest and vanilla sugar together.

- Now, carefully mix the egg white, yolk and flour together. The dough needs to be very light and airy.

- Heat up one or two pans and add butter once they are at medium heat.

- Add the dough and put raisins on top. Bake for 4-5 minutes on medium heat and then put into the oven until slightly brown. Remove from the oven and crush into small cubes using a knife and fork, dust with confectioner's sugar and put it back to the oven until it gets a little browner.

- Dust with confectioner's sugar and serve with the applesauce.

CURD CHEESE DUMPLINGS WITH STRAWBERRY SAUCE

TOPFENKNÖDEL MIT ERDBEERSAUCE ∗ SERVES 4

FOR THE DUMPLINGS

350 g	12 oz	curd cheese –"TOPFEN"– SEE PAGE 61 >>
100 g	3.5 oz	breadcrumbs
3 tbsp	3 tbsp	semolina/farina
3	3	eggs
30 g	1 oz	granulated sugar
zest of ½	zest of ½	organic lemon
a pinch	a pinch	salt and vanilla extract or sugar

FOR THE SAUCE

200 g	7 oz	strawberry
½-1 tbsp	½-1 tbsp	vanilla sugar or a pinch of vanilla

FOR THE BREADCRUMBS

65 g	2.3 oz	butter
120 g	4 oz	breadcrumbs
2 tbsp	2 tbsp	ground hazelnuts or almonds
1 tbsp	1 tbsp	granulated sugar
½ tsp	½ tsp	cinnamon powder

- FOR THE DUMPLINGS: Mix together all ingredients in a bowl and leave it sitting in fridge for at least 1 hour.
- FOR THE SAUSE: Put strawberries in a blender with a pinch of sugar, if desired.
- FOR THE ROASTED BREADCRUMBS: Melt the butter in a pan and add the breadcrumbs and nuts while stirring constantly. It will take up to 10-15 minutes on medium heat. Just never stop stirring or leave unattended. Add sugar and cinnamon.
- Heat up a larger pot with water and a little salt.
- Wet your hands and shape 12 small, evenly-shaped dumplings (4 cm / 1.5 inches) by hand and put them into the lightly simmering water. Cover the pan with a lid and allow to simmer for 7-10 minutes until they float to the surface.
- Take them out of the hot water with a slotted spoon and roll them in the warm bread crumbs.
- Enjoy your dumpling with strawberry sauce and roasted breadcrumbs.

VANILLA CRESCENTS
VANILLE KIPFERL * 35 PIECES

170 g	6 oz	baking flour
50 g	1.8 oz	ground nuts (almonds or hazelnuts)
a pinch	a pinch	salt
50 g	1.8 oz	confectioner's sugar, sifted
1/2 tbsp	1/2 tbsp	vanilla sugar – SEE PAGE 60 >>
100 g	3.5 oz	butter, cut into small pieces
1	1	egg yolk
1 tbsp	1 tbsp	cold cream or milk

USE ALL INGREDIENTS AT ROOM TEMPERATURE

FOR DECORATION

60 g	2 oz	confectioner's sugar mixed with vanilla powder

- Mix flour, nuts, salt, confectioner's sugar and vanilla sugar well in a bowl or on a working surface.

- Add butter and quickly mix, using a hand mixer or your hands, until all ingredients are well blended.

- Finally, add the egg yolk and cream to quickly make a smooth shortcrust pastry.

- Shape it into a ball and cover with clingfilm. Leave to sit in the fridge for at least 30 minutes or up to 2 days.

- Preheat your oven to 180°C / 355°F.

- Shape the pastry into a roll 1-2 cm/ 0.5 inches thick on a flour-dusted surface.

- Cut small slices off the dough and shape each slice into a crescent. Shape them from the inside to the outside, to create a fragile and beautiful crescent.

- Place them on a baking tray covered with baking paper.

- Bake the crescents for 5-7 minutes or until they turn slightly brown.

- Immediately roll them in vanilla sugar and leave to sit in a cookie tin for a week before serving.

This old Bohemian recipe is a must on every cookie plate – and the more fragile, the better the taste.

Austrian rum
makes a great gift for friends and family!

AUSTRIAN RUM BALLS
RUMKUGELN * 20-30 PIECES

60 g	2 oz	butter at room temperature
60 g	2 oz	confectioner's sugar, sifted
½ tbsp	½ tbsp	vanilla sugar – SEE PAGE 60 >>
		or a dash of vanilla extract
60 g	2 oz	ground hazelnuts
60 g	2 oz	ground coconut
60 g	2 oz	ground dark chocolate
2 tbsp	2 tbsp	Austrian rum
		>> If you prefer not to use alcohol, use fresh orange juice instead
2 tbsp		ground coconut or pumpkin seeds or cocoa powder
		paper molds

- Using a hand mixer, beat butter with confectioner's and vanilla sugar in a bowl until creamy.
- Mix in the hazelnuts, coconut, chocolate and rum.
- Place in the fridge for 30-60 minutes.
- Wet your hands, shape tiny balls and toss them in ground coconut or sprinkles.
- Place the Rum Balls in paper molds and leave them in the fridge or in a cool place until you serve them.

Austrian Rum

AUSTRIA is a landlocked country which has never had colonies with sugar cane plantations. Therefore, Austrians had to become creative to get over the shortage of rum, and in the 19th century a pharmacist near Vienna started to invent a recipe with alcohol and similar rum aroma.

Nowadays, the basic alcohol must be made of sugar cane and is only allowed to be produced in Austria. In fact, the Austrian rum has a very **distinctive flavor** of sweetness with hints of chocolate, which is intentionally used for AUSTRIAN SWEET DISHES, e.g. soaking raisins in rum or adding a dash of rum to the dough in order to get the flavor.

LINZER EYES

LINZER AUGEN * 15 PIECES

160 g	5.6 oz	baking flour
a pinch	a pinch	salt
50 g	1.8 oz	confectioner's sugar, sifted
½ tbsp	½ tbsp	vanilla sugar – SEE PAGE 60 >>
		or vanilla essence or powder
100 g	3.5 oz	butter, cut into small pieces
1	1	egg yolk
1 tbsp	1 tbsp	cream or milk
		redcurrant or apricot jam
		confectioner's sugar

USE ALL INGREDIENTS AT ROOM TEMPERATURE

- Mix flour, salt, confectioner's sugar and vanilla sugar well in a bowl or on a working surface.

- Add butter and quickly mix, using a hand mixer or your hands, until all ingredients are well blended.

- Finally, add egg yolk and cream to quickly make a smooth shortcrust pastry.

- Cover with clingfilm. Leave to sit in the fridge for at least 30 minutes or up to 2 days.

- Preheat your oven to 180° C / 355° F.

- Roll the pastry out to a thickness of 4 mm / 0.2 inch on a flour-dusted surface. Use round cutters. Cut 1-3 smaller holes into every second cookie.

- Bake the cookies for 5-7 minutes. Allow to cool on a rack.

- Warm up the jam slightly in a small pan, stirring occasionally.

- Put a little bit of jam in the middle of the base cookie without holes and cover it with the top cookie with holes.

- Leave it to sit for 1-2 hours so that they stick together perfectly.

- Dust with confectioner's sugar and store them in a cookie tin for a week before serving.

This recipe is named after the city of LINZ,
which is the capital of the region called "UPPER AUSTRIA"
and is located 200 km (124 miles) from Vienna.

Cookie cutter
the prefect
souvenir from
Vienna!

This is
the OLDEST RECIPE
which was carried to
France by an Armenian mule,
where it was spread to the
rest of THE WORLD.

GINGERBREAD COOKIES
LEBKUCHEN

FOR THE DOUGH

320 g	11 oz	rye flour
140 g	5 oz	cane sugar
2 tsp	2 tsp	baking soda
1 tsp	1 tsp	cocoa powder
1.5-2 tsp	1.5-2 tsp	gingerbread spice
2	2	eggs
80 g	3 oz	honey

FOR THE COATING & ICING

1	1	egg and a dash of milk
		halves of walnuts or peeled almonds
1	1	egg white
160-180 g	5.6-6.3 oz	confectioner's sugar, sifted
1	1	small freezer or pastry bag

- FOR THE DOUGH: Mix all ingredients well together in a bowl: it should be a moist, almost non-sticky dough.

- Shape into a ball and cover with clingfilm. Leave to sit in the fridge for 24 hours.

- Preheat your oven to 170° C / 340° F.

- Roll out the dough to a thickness of 0.5 cm / ¼ inch, on a flour-dusted surface.

- Use cookie cutters of your choice and place the cookies on a baking tray covered with baking paper.

- FOR THE COATING: Mix egg and milk well and only coat the gingerbread cookies lightly. Decorate with walnuts or almonds. Bake them for 6-8 minutes.

- FOR THE ICING: Put the egg white in a bowl and mix for 2 minutes, then gradually add sugar until the icing is thick and of smooth consistency.

- Fill a freezer bag with the icing, push the icing to one corner and cut a tiny bit off the corner. Decorate the cooled gingerbread cookies and leave them at room temperature until the icing has set hard.

- Store in a cookie tin with an apple to keep them moist.

HAZELNUT MACAROONS

HASELNUSSMAKRONEN

3	3	egg whites
		salt
70 g	2.5 oz	granulated sugar
1 tsp	1 tsp	vanilla sugar – SEE PAGE 60 >>
70 g	2.5 oz	confectioner's sugar
a pinch	a pinch	organic lemon zest and cinnamon
200 g	7 oz	ground hazelnuts
1	1	pastry bag
100 g	3.5 oz	chocolate
40 g	1.4 oz	butter

- Preheat your oven to 150° C/ 300° F.

- Whisk the egg whites with a pinch of salt in a bowl for 4 minutes until thickened. Slowly add granulated and vanilla sugar, until the egg whites can hold a peak.

- Now gently fold in confectioner's sugar, lemon zest, cinnamon and ground hazelnuts.

- Put the mixture into a pastry bag with a big round nozzle and pipe small circles or crescents onto a baking tray covered with baking paper.

- Bake the macaroons for 18-23 minutes, or until slightly brown. Allow to cool down completely on a rack.

- FOR THE GLAZE: Put pieces of chocolate and butter in a pan over another pan containing water simmering on a gentle heat and stir until smooth.

- When the chocolate has completely melted, allow to cool slightly before dipping the macaroons or drizzling chocolate onto the macaroons.

- Now allow to cool, until the chocolate has set hard.

- Store in an airtight container.

This is the perfect recipe for using up the egg whites after making the dough for
LINZER EYES, VANILLA CRESCENTS, BRABANTER
WALNUT COOKIES *and* EGG-YOLK KISSES.

BRABANTER WALNUT COOKIES

BRABANTER NUSSKEKS * 35 PIECES

200 g	7 oz	baking flour
80 g	2.8 oz	ground walnuts
a pinch	a pinch	salt, cinnamon and clove
70 g	2.5 oz	confectioner's sugar, sifted
1 tbsp	1 tbsp	vanilla sugar – SEE PAGE 60 >>
180 g	6.3 oz	butter, cut into small pieces
1	1	egg yolk
140 g	5 oz	redcurrant or apricot jam
100 g	3.5 oz	chocolate
40 g	1.4 oz	butter
35	35	walnut halves

USE ALL INGREDIENTS AT ROOM TEMPERATURE

- FOR THE DOUGH: Mix flour, nuts, spices, confectioner's sugar and vanilla sugar well in a bowl or on a working surface.

- Add the pieces of butter and mix quickly, using a hand mixer or your hands, until all ingredients are well blended.

- Finally add egg yolk to quickly make a smooth shortcrust pastry.

- Shape into a ball and cover with clingfilm. Leave to sit in the fridge for at least 30 minutes or up to 2 days.

- Preheat your oven to 180° C/ 355° F.

- Roll the pastry out to a thickness of 4 mm/ 0.2 inch on a flour-dusted surface and cut using round cookie cutters.

- Bake the cookies for 7 minutes or until they turn slightly brown. Allow to cool on a rack – carefully, as they are very fragile.

- In a small pan warm up the jam slightly, stirring occasionally.

- Put a little jam in the middle of one cookie and cover it with another cookie. Leave to sit for 1-2 hours so that they stick together perfectly.

- FOR THE GLAZE: Put pieces of chocolate and butter in a pan over another pan containing water simmering on a gentle heat and stir until smooth.

- Make sure that the cookies have stuck together and cooled down well; dip one side of the cookie into the chocolate and decorate with a walnut half on top.

- Now allow to cool, until the chocolate has set hard.

A melting kiss ...

EGG-YOLK KISSES
DOTTERBUSSERL

10	10	egg yolks
100 g	3.5 oz	confectioner's sugar, sifted
1 tbsp	1 tbsp	vanilla sugar – SEE PAGE 60 >>
a pinch	a pinch	salt
150 g	5.3 oz	baking flour
1	1	pastry bag
		apricot jam
130 g	4.5 oz	chocolate
60 g	2 oz	butter

> USE THE EGG WHITE FOR HAZELNUT MACAROONS

PREPARATION

- Preheat your oven to 180 °C/ 355 °F.

- Beat egg yolks in a bowl for 3-4 minutes with a hand mixer, before adding slowly sugar and salt, while constantly mixing until fluffy.

- Then gently fold in flour.

- Put the mixture into a pastry bag with a small round nozzle and pipe small circles onto a baking tray covered with baking paper. Leave some space between them.

- Bake them for 7 minutes or until slightly brown.
  Let them cool down on a rack.

- In a small pan, warm up the jam slightly, stirring occasionally.

- Using a teaspoon, put a little jam in the middle of one cookie and put another cookie on top. Leave them for 1-2 hours to get well stuck together.

- FOR THE GLAZE: Put pieces of chocolate and butter in a pan over another pan containing water simmering on a gentle heat and stir until smooth.

- When completely melted, dip one side of each Egg-Yolk Kiss in the icing.

- Allow to cool down until the chocolate has set hard.